ONE WISH

FRANCES WOLFE

Tundra Books

Published in Canada by Tundra Books,
481 University Avenue, Toronto, Ontario M5G 2E9

Published in the United States by Tundra Books of Northern New York,
P.O. Box 1030, Plattsburgh, New York 12901

Library of Congress Control Number: 2003111639

National Library of Canada Cataloguing in Publication

Wolfe, Frances
One wish / Frances Wolfe.

ISBN 0-88776-662-5

I. Title.

PS8595.O588O54 2003   jC813'.6   C2003-905079-3

We acknowledge the financial support of the Government of Canada
through the Book Publishing Industry Development Program and that of
the Government of Ontario through the Ontario Media Development
Corporation's Ontario Book Initiative. We further acknowledge the
support of the Canada Council for the Arts and the Ontario Arts
Council for our publishing program.

Design: Kong Njo

Medium: oil on Masonite

Printed in Hong Kong, China

1 2 3 4 5 6   08 07 06 05 04 03

For

Suzie and Jenny
Karin and Colleen
Kim
James
Emma and Taylor
Zachary and Noah

It is my wish that you will always possess
the heart to wish and the wisdom to know
that hard work will make wishes come true.

Love Fras

On a summer's
eve, a long
time ago,
I made one
wish on the
brightest star
in a twinkling
night sky.

I wished for a
cottage by the sea.
A cottage that
would stand in a
fragrant field of
Queen Anne's lace,
which would nod
and sway to a
melody only
it could hear.

My cottage would be yellow and have a sunny porch, wrapped in pink twining roses, where I could sit with a little friend on lazy afternoons.

On bright
blue mornings,
I would have
fancy tea parties
for a purr-fect
guest who
would lap
milk from a
china saucer.

Sometimes,
I would take a
small boat to the
shore to watch
her glide over
the cool,
clear water,
the wind
tugging at
her sails.

Or, I'd go
for a walk
on a long sandy
beach to feed
greedy gulls as
they fluttered
and screeched
all around me.

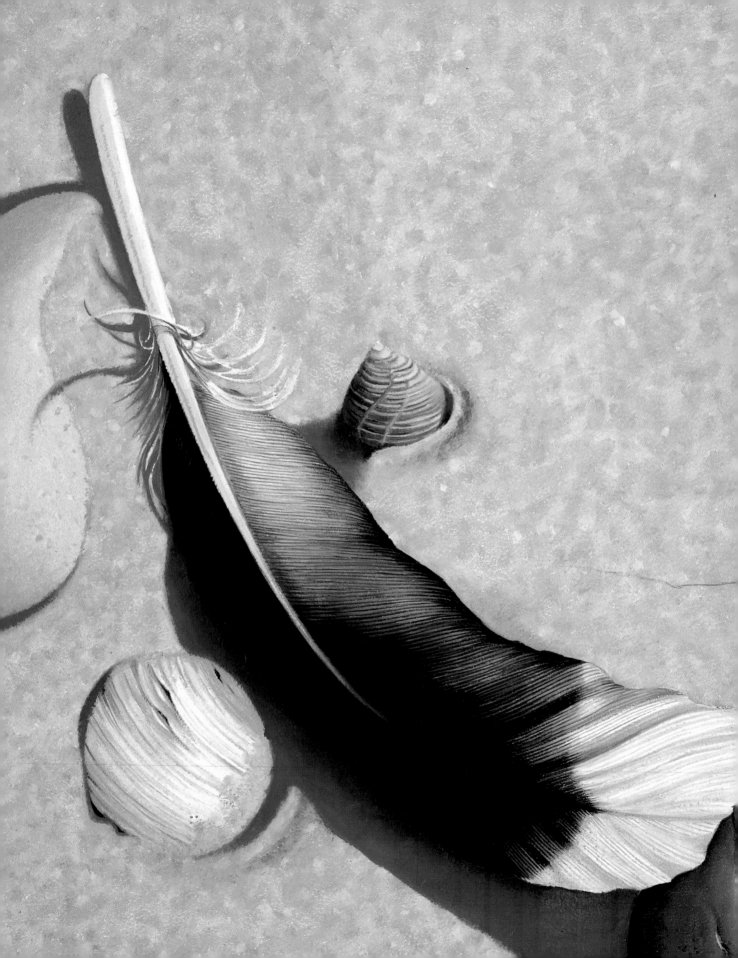

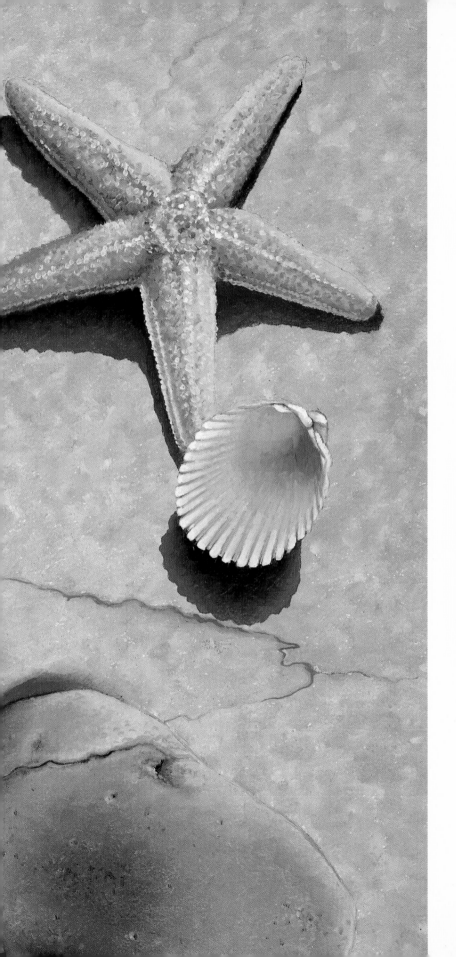

I would scavenge the beach for feathers, shells, and sea-worn stones, treasures delicately placed on the sand by the hand of the leaving tide.

◄O►◄O►◄O►◄O►◄O►◄O►◄O►

If the sun
got too warm,
I would take off
my clothes and
go for a swim.
I would splash
and play and let
the blue waves
wash over me.

With a bucket
and shovel, and
lots of wet sand,
I would build
a fine castle.
Then I would
watch as my castle
is conquered by
the coming tide.

If the cold
fog came
creeping,
I would
sit on a log
and listen to
the thundering
waves crash
on rumbling,
tumbling stones.

If I found
a seashell,
I would hold
it to my ear
to listen to
the sounds
of the sea,
trapped deep
in the chambers
of its spiral heart.

When I got hungry, I would go home to my cottage and have a great feast of clams, mussels, and lobster, delicious gifts from the bountiful sea.

And, at the
end of the day,
I would sit on
my porch and
watch the moon
rise up out of
the sea to join
the brightest star
in the twinkling
night sky.

The same star
I made one
wish upon
so many
years ago.
You see …

◄O►◄O►◄O►◄O►◄O►◄O►◄O►

Wishes

can come

true!